THE FARTING GINGERBREAD BUNNY

Once upon a time, there lived an old man and an old woman in a small house.

One day, the old woman decided to make a gingerbread bunny because Easter was just around the corner. She made the pastry, cut it, and put it in the oven.

While the gingerbread bunny was in the oven, the old man heard a loud sound. "What was that?" asked the old man, "It sounded like a fart!"

Just then, the oven door burst open. The gingerbread bunny ran out of the oven, farting loudly!

The old couple ran after the gingerbread
bunny. The bunny tried to hide in the grass.
But his farting gave him away.

"Get him!" cried the old man.
The bunny started running again.
He did not want to be eaten!

The gingerbread bunny ran across fields until he came to a cow.
"A gingerbread bunny!" yelled the cow. "He looks so tasty!"

Then, the cow started running after the bunny too! Every time the bunny tried to hide, his farting gave him away!

Then, the bunny ran past a fox.
"A gingerbread bunny!" yelled the fox, "Wait up!"
"Oh no!" cried the bunny as he ran, "You just want
to eat me!"

The fox ran after the bunny and finally caught up to him.
"Don't get close to me!" yelled the bunny,
"I'll fart!"

"Snap!" the fox's jaws closed right behind the bunny. The bunny was terrified! It made him fart louder than before!

The power of the fart made the bunny fly across the air! The old couple, the cow, and the fox stared at him in shock!

The gingerbread bunny landed on the soft grass. He looked around and saw a large, fluffy bunny staring at him

"I'm the Easter Bunny," said the large bunny,
"Why do you look so scared?"
"Everyone wants to eat me!" the gingerbread
bunny said while farting.

"And every time I try to hide, my farts give me away!" cried the gingerbread bunny. "Hmm..." said the Easter Bunny, thinking. "I think I can help you"

The Easter Bunny gave the Gingerbread Bunny a magical diaper. It made his farting sounds disappear!

"Thank you!" cried the gingerbread bunny,
"How can I repay you?"
"I'm very busy on Easter," said the Easter Bunny,
"Can you help me with my work?"

And so, together, they hopped away to deliver candy to kids and to hide Easter eggs.

From then on, every Easter, the gingerbread bunny helped the Easter Bunny. Together, they made a lot of kids happy!

The gingerbread bunny was also happy. He had finally found his place in the world!

Thanks

If you enjoyed this book
don't forget to give us a review
or a rating on Amazon.
It will be so much appreciated and
will help us create more
Amazing Books.

18805173R00021